Easy-to-Use
Object Lessons

Sheryl Bruinsma

Baker Book House
Grand Rapids, Michigan 49506

ISBN: 0-8010-0832-8

Sixth printing, August 1988

Printed in the United States of America

To
Uncle John Smilde

Contents

Index of Topics

How to Use This Book

Object lessons are a valuable way to present spiritual truths to children. Like the parables in the Bible, they make use of tangible objects to illustrate and reinforce Christian truths in a meaningful way. They are also a good way to hold children's attention.

The lessons in this book are appropriate for all school-aged children. When they are presented, the vocabulary can be adjusted to meet the needs of the children present. Some concepts are comparatively difficult to understand, so an approximate vocabulary and concept level has been indicated on each lesson. (Primary includes grades one to three; intermediate, grades three to five; junior high, grades five to eight).

To make these lessons easier to present, an outline has been included with each one. This outline will assist the speaker in remembering effective opening and closing remarks as well as a summary of the content. If necessary, the text can be read to the students. A complete section on how to give children's object lessons is included in my first book, *New Object Lessons for Children of All Ages*, published by Baker Book House in 1980.

To make this book as useful as possible it includes an index of topics as well as titles. Additional suggestions for similar objects that will illustrate the point are often given. Lessons have been arranged in order for a school year and many object lessons for special occasions (noted in the index of topics) have been included.

Family devotions are another effective way to use this material. The text for each lesson is written so that children can read the lessons to themselves or to each other.

1 Everybody Pull Together

(New Season)

Object:	A heavy bucket (weigh it down with bricks or sand). Thread, cut into two-foot lengths. The combined threads must be able to lift the weight of the bucket. You will also need three or four extra threads.
Suggestion:	For a small group, a length of thread can be cut for each child. The weight of the bucket can be adjusted so it can be lifted by the combined threads.
Lesson:	God wants all of us to work together for him.
Text:	"Help carry one another's burdens, and in this way you will obey the law of Christ" (Gal. 6:2).

Outline

Introduce object: This bucket is a heavy burden for someone to carry.

1. One thread—the load is borne by one person.
2. Two or three threads—some people will offer to help.
3. All of the threads together make it possible to easily lift the load.

Conclusion: Let's all lift the burden, get the project off the ground, and keep it going.

This bucket is a heavy burden for someone to carry. Perhaps that person has a big problem. It could be a meeting, a program, or a project. Watch what happens when one person tries to do this alone. (Attach one thread to the handle of the bucket and try to lift the bucket.) The thread breaks. This load is too heavy for just one person. It's not fair to expect one thread, or one person, to lift the load all alone. Do we sometimes expect the minister, the youth leader, the teacher, or one volunteer to carry the load by himself?

What about someone who has a big problem and could use our help? Sometimes a few people will offer their help. This is enough to lift a light load or get a small project going, but do you think a few threads will lift this bucket? (Attach two or three threads to the handle of the bucket and try to lift it.) No, these threads have broken, too. It seems that more than just a few helpers are needed.

Let's try putting everyone together. Pretend there is a thread here for each of you. Each one of you is important. Every person counts. When we all work together, we can easily carry one another's burdens. We can have successful programs. We can reach out to our neighbors with helpful projects.

Don't stand by watching. God wants you to help. Let's all lift the burden, get the project off the ground, and keep it going.

2 Joy in Giving to Others

Object: Glass containers of various sizes. A few balloons.

Lesson: To help others you must give of yourself. There are personal rewards in helping others.

Text: ". . . like the Son of Man, who did not come to be served, but to serve and to give his life to redeem many people" (Matt. 20:28).

Outline

Introduce object: Do you think I can pick up this glass without touching it with any part of my body? (Put balloon inside of the glass, blow up the balloon, and lift the glass.)

1. Pretend the glass is a person. You help him by giving of yourself, just as your breath fills the balloon and lifts the glass.
2. It is fun to try this experiment with different containers. There is joy in giving of yourself to others.
3. The more I lift the glasses, the easier it becomes.

Conclusion: Think of someone you could help.

Do you think I can pick up this glass without touching it with any part of my body? I can if I am willing to give of myself—my breath. (Demonstrate.) If this glass were a person, I could help him best by giving of myself also—my time, my concern, my sympathy, perhaps my money. What else could you give to help another person?

After I discovered this trick with the balloon, I went around my house trying to pick up containers of different sizes and shapes. It worked every time. It was a lot of fun to lift the glasses, and it made me realize that we can learn something else important from this. There is a reward—joy, happiness, contentment—that comes from knowing someone is happier because we took the time and trouble to help him. Jesus came to help others. We know he wants us to do the same. The amazing truth is that we are not just helping others but we also are gaining ourselves.

Usually I get short of breath and can't blow up more than two or three balloons at a time, but I was enjoying this experiment so much that I didn't run out of breath. When I forgot about myself, I could do more than I thought I could. This also happens when you are busy thinking about the needs of other people. Your own problems become smaller when you don't have time to think about them. Think of someone you could help.

3 What Things?

Object: A glass filled with marbles, coins, or other small objects. A container of tinted liquid.

Lesson: Fill your life with God and the things you possess will become unimportant.

Text: "Yes, may you come to know his love—although it can never be fully known—and so be completely filled with the very nature of God" (Eph. 3:19).

Outline

Introduce object: I have completely filled this glass with things.

1. People try to fill their lives with things, just as this glass is filled with things. Different people use different things.
2. Even when this glass is overflowing with things, it isn't full.
3. God can fill the empty spaces in our lives and even cover up or make unimportant the things in it.

Conclusion: Filling your life with things will not make it full.

I have completely filled this glass with things. I used marbles because we have a lot of them rolling around our house. The glass looks pretty full, doesn't it? Some of the marbles are even sticking up above the rim of the glass. Different people choose different things with which to fill their lives, but many of us have special things we have always wanted. We think we will be happy if we can get them. Some people figure that if they can collect or buy the latest things—toys, minibikes, cars, electronic games—their lives will be completely fulfilled. They long for and pine over this thing and that thing, thinking that when they get those things their lives will be full.

This glass may look full—filled to overflowing—but it really isn't. I have colored water in this pitcher. If the glass is really full, I won't be able to get another thing in it. Do you think I will be able to get any water into the glass? Yes, there seems to be quite a bit of room left in here. And look, the colored liquid is making the marbles seem dim—hard to see. Do you suppose there are also unfilled spaces in the lives of people who try to crowd their lives with things? The truth is, buying and owning things is never enough to fill a life and give happiness.

What can completely fill a life? Yes, the love of God—as our text says, "filled with the very nature of God." The best part is that when God fills your life the things in it become dim. They are no longer so important. It doesn't matter if something happens to them. We can say, "What things?" Let the love and presence of God fill your life. Remember, filling your life with things will not make it full.

4 A Prayer Answered

Object: A medium- or large-sized ball. A screen or large object (I used the balcony railing) that can hide a person who can catch and return the ball.

Lesson: Expect an answer to prayer.

Text: "If you believe, you will receive whatever you ask for in prayer" (Matt. 21:22).

Outline

Introduce object: Prayer is much like throwing a ball.

1. When you pray, expect an answer. (Throw the ball and have the hidden person return it.)
2. Sometimes you may feel that a prayer is not answered. (Throw the ball; have it returned but miss catching it.)
3. Sometimes you may feel that a prayer didn't reach God. (Throw the ball short of the target or in the wrong direction.)

Conclusion: The Bible tells us that if we pray sincerely, believing our prayers will be answered, they will be!

Prayer is much like throwing a ball, just as I am throwing this ball into the balcony. (The ball mysteriously returns.) Some people are as surprised when their prayers are answered as you were when this ball returned. Yet the Bible tells us that our sincere prayers will be answered—that we should expect an answer!

Sometimes you may feel that a prayer is not answered. (Throw the ball and fail to catch it when it returns.) There are times when we don't expect an answer and, therefore, miss it when it comes. Perhaps we walk away from it or go on to something else and miss the answer when it comes in God's time. We may no longer be looking for an answer or it may not come in the exact form that we are expecting. But the Bible tells us to look for an answer. God will answer our prayers.

Do you ever feel that your prayer hasn't reached God? There are times when we are not sincere or earnest about our prayers. We toss them up in God's general direction. (Throw the ball short of the target.) Our prayers become a form of ritual—we say them without paying much attention to what we are saying. What we need to do is to pray with energy and purpose. (Retrieve the ball and throw it again.)

The Bible tells us that if we pray sincerely, believing our prayers will be answered, they will be!

5 Faith Is Believing

Object: A calculator.

Lesson: Faith is believing and trusting in God.

Text: "To have faith is to be sure of the things we hope for, to be certain of the things we cannot see" (Heb. 11:1).

Outline

Introduce object: How many of you have ever used a calculator?

1. Trust the calculator. It works.
2. Use the calculator. It helps.
3. Keep the batteries in the calculator charged.

Conclusion: Your faith can lead you to become a successful Christian.

How many of you have ever used a calculator? There are three aspects of a calculator that remind me of faith. Faith is believing in God and his promises completely, knowing for sure that he loves you, trusting him for all you need to live and follow a Christian life. All of these things come from faith and lead back to it again.

Let's take a closer look at this calculator. It is a good one. I can perform several mathematical functions on it. When I push the buttons correctly, I can be sure of the answers—I can trust the answer to be correct. Faith needs to be used correctly and wisely, too. I know I can trust God and his promises. I know he is good and real and true. I know he loves me and takes care of me. If I can trust this little calculator, surely I can trust our great God!

This calculator won't do me much good if I don't use it. In fact, the more I use it, the better I become at pushing the buttons and getting the answers. The same is true of faith. The more you use it, the stronger it becomes. The more you trust God to help you, the easier a daily walk of faith becomes—the more things you find to trust him with and about. Faith works! The whole chapter of Hebrews 11 tells about people who used their faith to become successful Christians—Abraham, Jacob, Joseph, and Moses, to name a few.

Sometimes the batteries in this calculator run down and the figures become dim. Then I take the batteries out and put them into a recharger. Sometimes faith needs recharging. Even though faith doesn't run on batteries, it does run on something special supplied by God—free for the asking. Keep your faith charged—trust it, use it! Your faith can lead you to become a successful Christian.

6 Friendship

Object: An elastic bandage.

Lesson: The biblical view of friendship.

Text: "Friends always show their love. What are brothers for if not to share trouble?" (Prov. 17:17).

Outline

Introduce object: Part of growing up is falling down. When you fall, you often need a bandage.

1. This bandage is there in time of trouble.
2. The bandage supports and protects you.
3. The bandage still allows you to move and be yourself.
4. This bandage stretches—it has give and take—and can go over bumps and around corners.

Conclusion: The Bible says a friend loves at all times. Are you this kind of a friend?

Part of growing up is falling down. When you fall, you often need a bandage. When you bleed, you need a regular bandage; when you sprain your arm or leg, you need one of these special elastic bandages. True friendship—the kind that matches the biblical view of friendship—is like this bandage.

First of all, a true friend is there when you need a friend, especially in time of trouble (just as this elastic bandage is ready when you have a physical problem). A true friend doesn't take off when the going gets tough.

This elastic bandage supports the injured arm or leg and protects it from more bumps. A friend will offer words of support and encouragement. He will protect his friend from difficult situations.

An interesting thing about this bandage is that, when you use it, it moves when you move. It is not like a stiff cast that won't bend and confines your limb so that it becomes uncomfortable. A true friend wants to be a helpful companion but doesn't suffocate a person. True friendship allows you to move and be yourself.

Finally, this bandage stretches so that it can go over bumps and around corners. Friendship stretches to cover unusual situations and unexpected events. Friends show their love and concern always. The Bible says a friend loves at all times. Are you this kind of a friend?

7 A Flight to Heaven

Object: A model of a rocket, a toy rocket, or a picture or a drawing of a rocket.

Lesson: Death is like a flight to heaven.

Text: "And after I go and prepare a place for you, I will come back and take you to myself, so that you will be where I am" (John 14:3).

Outline

Introduce object: Rocket travel may be the thing of the future but thinking about actually traveling by rocket is a bit scary.

1. The destination, when we die, is life eternal with Jesus.

2. Death is a trip all people will make sooner or later. The quality of our life, not the quantity of it, is what counts.

3. Some people are afraid to die.

    a. They leave their family and friends behind.

    b. They are afraid of the unknown.

Conclusion: I don't want to die but I am not afraid because I know I will go to where Jesus is. My life will be different, but it will be better!

Rocket travel may be the thing of the future but actually thinking about traveling by rocket is a bit scary. It would be a great adventure, but I don't know much about rocket travel. Thinking about taking a trip in this rocket will help you think about death.

We could imagine that this rocket is going to another planet. What is our destination when we die? We go to our heavenly home to spend forever—eternity—with Jesus. I don't know too much about what heaven will be like, but I don't know much about living on other planets, either.

Unlike a rocket trip, death is a trip all people will make sooner or later. Some people live a long time. Others die sooner. It is not how long we live that matters but what kind of life we live in the time Jesus gives us. He gives us all as much time as we need to live for him.

Some people would be afraid to take a rocket trip to a far-off planet. The trip would be long and dangerous. Some people are afraid to die because they don't want to leave their friends and family. They don't want to go to an unknown place or travel in a strange rocket. I don't want to die but I am not afraid because I know I will go to where Jesus is. My life will be different, but it will be better.

8 Good Grief!

Object: An onion, a knife, and a container.

Lesson: Grief is an important and positive emotion.

Text: "Happy are you who weep now; you will laugh" (Luke 6:21b).

Outline

Introduce object: When I peel this onion, it makes me cry.

1. What is grief?
2. Why do we grieve?
3. What does grief accomplish?

Conclusion: This onion is still making me cry but the tears are washing the irritating oil out of my eyes. Let real tears help clean the grief from our hearts. Then trust God to help us get on with our lives!

When I peel this onion, it makes me cry. The oil spraying out from this onion irritates my eyes and produces tears. Tears can mean a lot of things. They come when you are very excited, when you laugh too hard, when you are tired or upset, when you are hurt, or when you are sad.

When we have a deep sadness that causes us emotional suffering we call that emotion grief. We hear a lot about happiness, love, joy, peace, anger, jealousy, and hatred. We don't talk much about grief, but it is a very real emotion that we all experience at one time or another.

Different things cause us grief. We grieve when someone important to us dies. We grieve when a pet dies. We grieve when we are really sorry for something we have done. We grieve when we lose an important friendship. When we grieve, we cry hard and that is good for us. Crying helps relieve our severe sorrow. God made us so that we can express this grief and then, when we have cried, realize that we have to pick ourselves up, start our lives again, and trust God to know what is best for us. Expressing grief helps us get over our loss.

Sometimes we grieve for things we can do something about. When we have done something wrong and we feel sorry, we can set about to make it right. Grief leads to repentance—telling God that we are sorry. Then he forgives us. We may need to apologize to someone or do something else to right the wrong. When grief leads us into action it is also a good thing.

This onion is still making me cry but the tears are washing the irritating oil out of my eyes. Let real tears help clean the grief from our hearts. Then trust God to help us get on with our lives!

9 It's Not What You Have But What You Are

Object: Bubbles. Available in the toy department, this jar of liquid comes with a stick with a ring on one end. The ring is dipped into the liquid. When you blow through the ring, bubbles float out into the room. (Broken toys can be used also—alone or with the bubbles.)

Lesson: Materialism.

Text: "Keep your lives free from the love of money, and be satisfied with what you have" (Heb. 13:5a).

Outline

Introduce object: Can you tell me what toy you wanted most a year ago? Here is something I wanted as a child.

1. The things we have on earth are temporary. They pop like bubbles.
2. The Bible doesn't say we shouldn't have things, but that we must put them in their proper place of importance.

Conclusion: It's not what you have but what you are that counts.

Can you tell me what toy you wanted most a year ago? Here is something I wanted as a child. Most of you have seen these bubbles before—but not in church! Let's see if I can still blow bubbles. Yes, and aren't they neat! Too bad they don't last long.

Most of the things we have don't last very long. The Bible says they are temporary, which means that we have them only for a time. We all know that things—toys, belongings—get used up like these bubbles that pop so quickly, or spill, or break, or get lost. We may get tired of things or put them away and forget about them. We have or use them for only a short time and they should not be too important to us. Could you remember what you wanted a year ago when I just asked? Probably not.

The Bible doesn't say we should not have things at all, but that we should remember that they are not what is important in life. What really matters is what kind of a person you are. You don't need things to be happy. The secret is realizing this, being content with what we have, and spending our energy developing the things that are important—loving, sharing with and helping others, deepening our Christian commitment, and enjoying Jesus' love, peace, and joy. Then we are collecting heavenly treasures that will last.

It's not what you have but what you are that counts.

10 Catch!

Object: Someone who has a bad cold or pretends to have a bad cold. (Drawings of people with measles, mumps, and chicken pox can be used if desired.)

Lesson: The Bible cautions us about carefully choosing our companions.

Text: "Do not be fooled. 'Bad companions ruin good character'" (I Cor. 15:33).

Outline

Introduce object: There are many things we can catch from our friends. A-choo! Excuse me. This cold is one of them.

1. Physical—colds, flu, measles, mumps, or chicken pox.
2. Spiritual—bad habits, attitudes, and actions.

Conclusion: Choose friends you want to be like—because you will!

There are many things we can catch from our friends. A-choo! Excuse me. This cold is one of them. A generous student shared it with me. I'll have to be careful or my family and friends will catch it from me. I have some drawings of other things you can catch from friends— measles, mumps, chicken pox. You can get shots to help keep you from getting measles and mumps but the only thing you can do for chicken pox, colds, and some kinds of flu is to get them. The only way you can try to avoid them— a-choo! excuse me—is to stay away from the germs.

There are other things you can catch from people—bad habits, attitudes, and actions. There are no shots that will protect you from getting them. The Bible warns us that bad companions will have an effect on our character. If you choose to associate with people who have poor attitudes, you will find your own attitudes slowly changing—perhaps so slowly you don't even notice it. It took this cold a few days to incubate or get bad enough to show symptoms— make me feel and act sick. It could take your habits, attitudes, and actions weeks to begin to show symptoms. Often even these symptoms are ignored until it is too late.

It is very, very important to choose your friends carefully. Choose friends you want to be like—because you will!

11 Count Your Blessings

(Thanksgiving)

Object: A child's pet, such as a hamster.

Lesson: We have much for which to thank God.

Text: "Let us come before him with thanksgiving and sing joyful songs of praise" (Ps. 95:2).

Outline

Introduce object: We are thankful to God all year long, but Thanksgiving is a season set apart to count our blessings, to think of as many things as we can to thank God for, and to spend time in sincere, thankful prayer. Perhaps this little hamster can help us think of even more things for which we can be thankful.

1. Thinking about what a hamster needs to live helps us to remember how God supplies our needs.
2. This hamster is just one part of God's creation. It leads us to be grateful for all of creation.
3. We love our pets. They add joy to our lives. We can thank God for our spiritual blessings.

Conclusion: The world is so big and God is so good. This little hamster has made us only begin to think. What more can you think of for which you can be thankful?

We are thankful to God all year long, but Thanksgiving is a season set apart to count our blessings, to think of as many things as we can to thank God for, and to spend time in sincere, thankful prayer. Perhaps this little hamster can help us think of even more things for which we can be thankful. It is easy for us to forget about some of the things that are necessary for life—we take them for granted. Think for a minute about what this hamster needs to live. It needs food, water, a clean and safe cage, protection, and exercise. You need similar things—perhaps not a cage but a clean and safe place to live nevertheless. Do you have these things? Do you know that there are children in the world who do not have enough food to eat, who must live in dirty, unhealthy places, who often do not have someone to teach and protect them, who wear torn and dirty clothes, who get diseases so that they suffer constantly and cannot grow properly? Thank you, God, for giving us all of these things that make our lives safe and healthy and comfortable.

God has made this little hamster so perfectly. It is bright-eyed, active, and a lot of fun to watch. It reminds us to thank God for all of his wonderful creation—animals, flowers, plants, trees, lakes, mountains, softly falling rain or snowflakes, warm sunshine, floating clouds. What do you enjoy most about God's wonderful creation?

We love our pets. They bring joy to our lives. We can thank God for meeting all of our spiritual needs—love, peace, joy, fellowship, trust, comfort, sharing, caring, strength, happiness.

The world is so big and God is so good. This little hamster has made us only begin to think. What more can you think of for which you can be thankful?

12 The Ladder of Success

Object: A paper ladder. To make a paper ladder, roll a piece of paper (newsprint will do). Cut a section out of the top middle, as shown in the diagram. Bend the edges down and pull the center pieces straight out. A little practice will make this easy to do.

Lesson: To have a fuller life you must think less of yourself and reach out to others.

Text: ". . . but be humble toward one another, always considering others better than yourselves. And look out for one another's interests, not just for your own" (Phil. 2:3b–4).

Outline

Introduce object: Watch carefully and I'll make a ladder from this piece of paper.

1. We need to pull ourselves together. (Roll up the paper.)
2. We need to give up our self-centeredness. (Cut out the center piece of the paper.)
3. We need to reach out to others and up to God. (Pull the paper straight up and out.)

Conclusion: We are reaching, climbing, stretching, and gaining a broader perspective and a fuller Christian life.

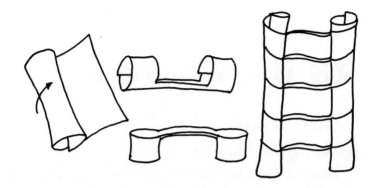

Watch carefully and I'll make a ladder from this piece of paper. First I roll it up into a nice neat tube. As Christians seeking fuller lives, we first have to pull ourselves together— to get our act together, to keep from spreading ourselves too thin or in too many different directions, to tighten our control of our lives. Christians are not wishy-washy, free-floating, goalless people. They have purpose and direction to their lives. That direction is loving and serving God and helping other people.

In order to do this—to serve God and to help our fellow men—we need to think less about ourselves. I am cutting out the middle of this tube, just as we must cut the selfishness out of our lives. Now there is less of self. The person is no longer self-centered. When we are busy thinking about others we do not have time to worry about our own selfish interests. God meets our needs for us. We do not have to be constantly thinking about them and distorting them.

Finally, to complete the ladder, I bend down the sides and pull straight out. The final step in having a fuller Christian life is to reach up and out—up to God and out to other people, so fulfilling God's purpose for us. As we help to meet the needs of others, our lives are enriched. We are reaching, climbing, stretching, and gaining a broader perspective and a fuller Christian life.

13 Alone, Yet Together

Object: A music box.

Lesson: Two aspects of worship—solitude and togetherness.

Text: "Christ is like a single body, which has many parts; it is still one body, even though it is made up of different parts" (I Cor. 12:12).

Outline

Introduce object: How many of you have ever seen the machine that makes music inside of a music box? (Explain how the mechanism works.)

1. We worship alone—side by side.

2. We worship together—each note is important to the song.

Conclusion: Let's worship God alone, yet together.

How many of you have ever seen the machine that makes music inside of a music box? If you look carefully, you can see a metal cylinder with bumps on it. This cylinder turns when the music box is wound up and the bumps pluck these pieces of metal standing side by side next to the cylinder. The pieces of metal are different lengths. The short ones sound with high notes. As the metal pieces get longer, the notes get lower. The bumps are placed on the cylinder so that they will pluck the notes in the right order to produce a song.

When we worship, we stand alone—each of us different as the metal pieces are different. We stand side by side but each of us has his own different note to play. When we worship, we pray, sing, and commune with God as individuals who stand one to one with our God and Savior. We can worship alone in this way, but it is often easier or meaningful in a different way to worship at the same time—alone, yet side by side.

Another important type of worship takes place when we worship together with every person contributing, just as all of the notes of the music box are important to the song. We pray together, sing together, love God together, and learn from each other. Together we can make beautiful music.

God made us so that we can worship alone with him. He also wants us to join together to love and praise him. Let's worship God alone, yet together.

14 Get Involved in the Game

(Christmas)

Object: An electronic game.

Lesson: The spirit of Christmas comes from within. It is the necessary element in the celebration of Christmas.

Text: ". . . the shepherds said to one another, 'Let's go to Bethlehem and see this thing that has happened, which the Lord has told us.' So they hurried off and found Mary and Joseph and saw the baby lying in the manger" (Luke 2:15b–16; also read Luke 2:14).

Outline

Introduce object: Electronic games are very popular. This one is going to help me tell you about the most important part of celebrating the birth of Christ, Christmas—the spirit of Christmas.

1. What is the spirit of Christmas? It is the feeling of joy, peace, and good will that we have when we turn on or tune in to the real meaning of Christmas. (Turn on the game.)

2. How do we get the spirit of Christmas? We get it when we become involved, just as we must push the buttons to play the game.

Conclusion: Just as the shepherds hurried to Bethlehem to see what the angels had told them about, so must we join in, get involved, show the spirit of Christmas.

Electronic games are very popular. This one is going to help me tell you about the most important part of celebrating the birth of Christ, Christmas—the spirit of Christmas. What is the spirit of Christmas? It is the feeling of joy, peace, and good will we have when we remember Christ's birth. The real spirit comes from within us—each of us individually. It affects what we do to celebrate Christmas. This electronic game is interesting-looking but it will do nothing unless I turn it on. So, too, you must make a decision to join in—turn on—to the real meaning of Christmas. Otherwise the celebration of Christmas will go on about you and you may join in other aspects of it, but you may miss the true meaning and the true joy of the season.

Many things go on at Christmas time that sidetrack people. For example, some people spend most of their time thinking about themselves and what they want to get from others at Christmas. Often this leaves them disappointed. That is like turning the game on and expecting it to play by itself. You need to push the buttons, be active. Then the game flashes lights and makes beeping sounds. You need to reach out to others, bring happiness, give of yourself and your time, enjoy all of the symbols and remembrances of the season—truly celebrate the birth of Jesus.

The celebration of Christmas may go on about you, but the true spirit of Christmas comes from within and reaches out to those around us. Just as the shepherds hurried to Bethlehem to see what the angels had told them about, so must we join in, get involved, show the spirit of Christmas.

15 A Fresh Start

(New Year's)

Object: A new box of crayons.

Lesson: A new year symbolizes a fresh start—a chance to grow, to help, and to become a better Christian.

Text: "Create a pure heart in me, O God, and put a new and loyal spirit in me" (Ps. 51:10).

Outline

Introduce object: To me there has always been something exciting about a new box of crayons.

1. Like the new year, these crayons have never been used.

2. As we make promises to ourselves about new crayons, so we make promises about the new year.

3. New crayons give us the material to draw all kinds of interesting pictures. The new year gives us a chance to live and do and be more.

Conclusion: God is giving you a new year. What will you do with it?

To me there has always been something exciting about a new box of crayons. These crayons are pointed, unbroken, unused. So, too, is the new year. God forgives us every time we come to him and say we are sorry. Every day with him can be new. However, it is a good reminder for us to use a certain time of year as a time to think especially about a new and fresh beginning. The beginning of the new year is a perfect time for this.

Every time I open a new box of crayons I think, "Now, I'm not going to break any of these new crayons. I'll be careful not to lose them, either. I'll keep the paper unripped unless I have to carefully peel it down a little." When the new year begins, we make promises about what we will do with it. These are called new year's resolutions. A person may resolve, "I will do my best to always finish my homework" or "I will clean my room before my mother yells at me."

We can do even more with the new year. A new box of crayons gives us the material to draw all kinds of interesting pictures. It is easier and more fun to draw with fresh, pointed, unbroken crayons. In the same way, the start of a new year can be the beginning of a new adventure—a chance to live and do and be more, a chance to dream up ways to help other people, a chance to grow and become a better Christian.

God is giving you a new year. What will you do with it?

16 A Star to Follow

(Epiphany)

Object: Several stylized representations of a star.

Lesson: Follow what leads you to Jesus.

Text: "And asked, 'Where is the baby born to be the king of the Jews? We saw his star when it came up in the east, and we have come to worship him'" (Matt. 2:2).

Outline

Introduce object: We have many ways of making stars to remind us of the star that led the wise men in search of Jesus.

1. Our purpose, like that of the wise men, is to find the king.

2. Our goal is to worship the king, as the wise men did.

Conclusion: We all need a goal, a purpose, a star to follow!

We have many ways of making stars to remind us of the star that led the wise men in search of Jesus. These are some of our stars—but what was their star like? Modern astronomers think it was a crossing of planets in a certain part of the sky. We think the wise men were early astronomers who spent much time watching the heavens and studying the stars. Epiphany is a special time of the year. We think about the wise men because they have so much to teach us. They started following the star about the time Jesus was born and needed as much as two years to find him—including a stop to ask Herod for directions.

Why did the wise men follow the star? They were excited about what they saw. The star meant a baby was born to be the king of the Jews. The wise men had a purpose—to find the king. They made a long and difficult trip to accomplish this purpose. We, too, need a firm purpose to find our king. We can't follow the original star, but there still are ways that lead to Jesus—special people in our lives, going to church, praying, and reading the Bible.

What did the wise men do when they found the king? They worshiped him. We worship him today. That is what we are doing right now. Think for a minute about how the wise men must have felt when they finally found the baby after such a long and difficult search. Can we worship with as much feeling as they must have had? They knew only of a baby. We know that baby grew up, died for us, and loves us today. We have even more reason to worship him with deep feeling, excitement, and reverence.

We all need a goal, a purpose, a star to follow!

17 It's What's Inside That Counts

Object: Unwaxed paper cups, a candle, and a bowl of water.

Lesson: The love of Jesus inside us helps us in our treatment of others.

Text: "To your godliness add brotherly affection; and to your brotherly affection add love" (II Peter 1:7; read vv. 3–8).

Outline

Introduce object: What happens when a paper cup is held over a candle flame?

1. People get so angry sometimes that, like this cup, they burn up. (Hold an empty cup over the flame. The cup will smolder and burn.)

2. When you have the love of Jesus inside you, he will help you not to burn. (Hold a cup filled with water over the flame. This cup will not burn.)

Conclusion: It's what's inside that counts!

What happens when a paper cup is held over a candle flame? Would you like me to try it so you can find out? Pretend that you are this cup and the flame is something that is happening to make you angry. Perhaps someone has said something mean to you, taken your turn, or broken your toys. When this happens to the cup (hold it over the flame), it starts to smoke. Now it is beginning to burn. I'll have to put it out quickly. (Put the cup in the bowl of water.) Do you ever become so angry that you feel like you are burning up? Sometimes we even hear people say, "That burns me up!"

I have another cup here. Would you like me to try again? (Have a second cup, with water in it, ready.) This one doesn't seem to be burning. Why not? There is water in this cup. It keeps the paper cool so that it won't burn. Are you surprised that this second cup isn't burning? It is getting a little black from the candle flame, but it is definitely not burning. Why not? There is something in this cup that is keeping it cool—water. What can we have inside of us that will keep us cool? Yes, Jesus' love for us and our love for him helps us keep our cool. Jesus gives so much love that it spills from us onto other people. This does not mean that you will never become angry again. There are some things that should upset us, such as seeing a bully picking on a little child or hearing someone take God's name in vain. But the love of Jesus in us will help keep us from burning up or striking out at other people in an unkind or unwise way. We love Jesus and we know that he wants us to be kind to other people. This love is powerful. It's what's inside that counts!

43

18 Read It!

Object: A musical instrument (I used a piano) and a lesson book for the instrument.

Lesson: Read and study the Bible.

Text: "They listened to the message with great eagerness, and every day they studied the Scriptures . . ." (Acts 17:11b).

Outline

Introduce object: Once upon a time a child had an old piano and wanted to learn how to play it. Since there was no money for lessons, a friend gave the boy a lesson book and said, "Here is a book that will help you."

1. Set the lesson book on the piano. (Leave the Bible on a table.)

2. Open the book. (Leave the Bible open without reading it.)

3. Read the book and study it. (Read and study the Bible; apply what you learn.)

Conclusion: The Bible doesn't do you any good if it's closed, or open and unread. You need to read it, study it, and live by it!

Once upon a time a child had an old piano and wanted to learn how to play it. Since there was no money for lessons, a friend gave the boy a lesson book and said, "Here is a book that will help you." The boy took the book home and set it on the piano. He started banging on the keys. His banging, however, wasn't any better than it had been before he got the book, so he went back to his friend and told him that the book didn't work. When the friend found out what the boy had done he said, "Nothing will happen if you don't even open the book!"

The boy went home, opened the book, placed it on the piano, and started banging on the keys again. Still nothing special happened, so he went back to his friend and told him that the book still didn't work. This time his friend said, "Did you read it? Did you do what it told you to do?"

The boy went home and opened the book to the first lesson. He read it carefully and did exactly what it said to do. Soon he was able to play a little tune.

The same is true of the Bible. It is an important part of learning about the Christian life, but many people leave the Bible closed, thinking that just having it on a table where they can see it will help them. Sometimes they will open it or page through it without reading it. It doesn't help you to have a Bible unless you read it regularly, study it, ask God to make it meaningful to you, let it inspire and direct you, and spend quiet time thinking about what it says. The Bible doesn't do you any good closed, or open and unread. You need to read it, study it, and live by it!

19 Going Places

Object: Three inflatable balloons, a straw, tape, and string. (Two balloons are to be allowed to fly at random around the room; one balloon is to be attached to the straw with tape. The straw has been threaded onto a string that has been attached to a distant object. When this balloon is released, it will be propelled along the string toward the distant goal. For a surprise element, use thread or nylon fishing line that cannot be seen, so the balloon will appear to travel along an invisible path.)

Lesson: Have Christian goals and direction in your life.

Text: "Wise people walk the road that leads upward to life . . ." (Prov. 15:24a). "Keep walking in straight paths . . ." (Heb. 12:13a).

Outline

Introduce object: People are like balloons—filled with energy, ready to be out in life.

1. It is easy to be busy going around in circles. (Let two balloons fly free.)
2. God has a plan and direction for our lives. (Release the balloon on the straw; this balloon travels in a straight path.)

Conclusion: If you really want to go places that count, you need God's direction in your life.

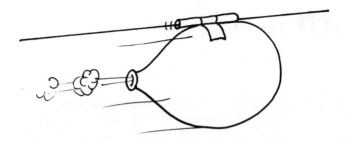

People are like balloons—filled with energy, ready to be out in life. This balloon is ready to fly around. Watch it go. (Let a balloon fly free.) It is easy for people to be busy going around in circles, darting this way and that, using up all of their energy without accomplishing much, plunging head-long in this direction and that one. Not all people dart in the same direction. (Release another balloon.) These two balloons do have one thing in common—they fly around a lot but don't really accomplish much.

We don't need to live our lives this way. God has a plan and direction for our lives. However, we have to attach our-selves to his plan. I'm going to tape this balloon to the straw and let it go. Look at that balloon go straight to the far corner of the room. We can lead productive lives with our energy directed toward our Christian goals—bringing love and peace to those around us. Living and learning Christ's example, directing ourselves toward Christian commitment, seeking to please God and follow his plan for our lives are ways to direct our energy into a straight and useful life.

If you really want to go places, you need God's direction in your life.

20 Have a Heart

(Valentine's Day)

Object: A large valentine with a heart on it, a realistic model of a heart, or a paper heart.

Lesson: When the Bible talks about the heart, it means the center of our spiritual existence, our emotions—especially love.

Text: "And I pray that Christ will make his home in your hearts through faith. I pray that you may have your roots and foundation in love" (Eph. 3:17).

Outline

Introduce object: Why do we use the symbol of a heart on a valentine?

1. The heart is necessary for physical life. The word *heart* refers to the center of spiritual life—especially love.

2. The heart is hard-working. Love is hard-working (I Cor. 13:4-5).

3. The heart is faithful. Love is faithful (I Cor. 13:5-7).

Conclusion: How can we have this kind of love? God made us in his image, with the capacity to love. Sometimes we need extra help from him to love more completely. We can let him love others through us.

Why do we use the symbol of a heart on a valentine? What does it mean when we say, "Have a heart?" What does the Bible mean when it talks about the heart?

We know that we cannot live without a heart. In fact, many people die from heart attacks. Our heart is necessary for our physical life. In a similar way, the word *heart* is often used in the Bible to talk about the most important part of our spiritual lives—the part of us that thinks and feels, our emotions, especially love. Love is so necessary that doctors tell us a baby will not grow and develop into a healthy, happy adult without love. A person who is not loved or who cannot love others is sad and lonely. Knowing about and sharing in the love of God is the most exciting thing we can do in life.

The heart is hard-working. It pumps about five quarts of blood per minute. The heart squeezes or contracts seventy to eighty times a minute. Love is hard-working also. Sometimes people we love do unlovable things. Some people are not easy to love. I Corinthians 13:4–5 tells us "love is patient and kind; it is not jealous or conceited or proud; . . . love does not keep a record of wrongs."

The heart is faithful. It keeps right on working, whatever we are doing, whether we are thinking about it or not. It beats more than 2.5 billion times in an average lifespan of seventy years. The Bible tells us that love is faithful as well. "Love never gives up; and its faith, hope, and patience never fail" (I Cor. 13:7). Love forgives. You are loved for what you are and you love others in the same way.

How can we have this kind of love? God made us in his image, with the capacity to love. Sometimes we need extra help from him to love more completely. We can let him love others through us.

21 Be Patient

Object: A heavy stack of books placed on one end of a piece of paper large enough so that, when the paper is pulled slowly from the other end, the stack of books will move.

Lesson: God desires us to learn patience.

Text: "Be patient and wait for the LORD to act . . ." (Ps. 37:7 a).

Outline

Introduce object: How many of you think I can move this stack of books without touching it?

1. Pull the paper quickly—the books don't move.

2. Pull the paper slowly and patiently—the books move.

Conclusion: Patience means getting things in God's time, not ours.

How many of you think I can move this stack of books without touching it? Let's see. That sounds pretty tough. The books are on this piece of paper—I'll try to move them by pulling on the paper. (Yank the paper from under the books.)

That didn't work. I must have done something wrong. (Replace the paper.) I guess I need to have more patience. What is patience? It is waiting for what God has planned for you. Sometimes it is difficult to wait—for example, if you wait for ice cubes to melt so you can have a drink when you are thirsty. When we want something, we want it now? Sometimes patience means enduring something unpleasant, without complaining, until we get what we want or something better. Sometimes patience means doing things slowly, carefully, deliberately—thinking, planning, and considering God's way.

Slowly and deliberately. I'll try pulling this paper carefully. Yes, when I pull slowly, the books stay on the paper and I can move them without touching them. Often, everybody has to wait for something important in his life. It could be recovering from an illness or accident. It could be waiting for a party or some special event. It is not easy to wait, but if you practice having patience, waiting gets easier. Remind yourself that everything will come in God's own time and the waiting will become less troublesome. Direct your energy toward something more useful than complaining about the waiting.

Patience means getting things in God's time, not ours.

22 Encircling Love

(Lent)

Object: A piece of paper six inches square. As you talk, fold the paper in half and cut across from the fold to within a half-inch of the other edge. Turn the paper over and cut from the outside to the fold, again stopping within a half-inch from the folded edge. Keep making cuts, from opposite sides and about a half-inch apart. End with a cut that begins on the folded side. Cut along the fold from point A to point B, being careful not to cut the two outside strips. Open. (Practice on scrap paper.)

Lesson: The greatness of God's love.

Text: "For God so loved the world, that he gave his only begotten Son, that whosoever believeth in him should not perish, but have everlasting life" (John 3:16, KJV).

Outline

Introduce object: Do you think this piece of paper can be cut to make an unbroken piece large enough to fit over your head?

1. This piece of paper can be cut in a special way so that it will fit. What can you think of that will fit in this room but is big enough to cover the whole world? (God's love; Jesus' sacrifice.)

2. This paper looks like a decoration. We decorate to prepare for a big party. Lent is the season of the year when we prepare for and think about Jesus' sacrifice for us.

Conclusion: In this special time of year, let us give extra thought to the greatness of God's love and the unsurpassed sacrifice of Jesus.

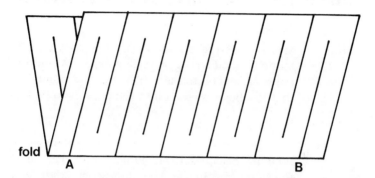

fold A B

Do you think this piece of paper can be cut to make an unbroken piece large enough to fit over your head? If I fold this paper over and make a few cuts here and there, I do have a long connected strip of paper that will fit. What can you think of that will fit in this room but is big enough to cover the whole world? God's love is the only thing I know of that is so great, so limitless. It was big enough to allow him to send his own son to die for us. Jesus' love is so great that he wanted to make this sacrifice for us.

This cut paper bounces when I hold it up. It looks like a decoration. We use decorations like this for parties or special events. We put them up to prepare for a celebration. We also prepare or plan ahead for the time of year when we remember Jesus' sacrifice for us. We call the season of preparation Lent. We prepare our hearts and minds. Many people make sacrifices—give up candy or other things for Lent—to help them remember Jesus' great love and sacrifice.

In this special time of year, let us give extra thought to the greatness of God's love and the unsurpassed sacrifice of Jesus.

23 Do You Have a Watermark?

Object: Samples of paper containing a watermark (usually found in good typing or writing paper). When the paper is held up to the light, a name or number that has been pressed into the paper can be seen.

Lesson: Baptism.

Text: "Go, then, to all peoples everywhere and make them my disciples: baptize them in the name of the Father, the Son, and the Holy Spirit" (Matt. 28:19).

Outline

Introduce object: Does this look like a plain, empty piece of paper? It's not. When I hold it up to the light, I can see some marks. (Explain the watermark.)

1. Baptism is our watermark.
2. Our trademark is "in the name of the Father, the Son, and the Holy Spirit," showing that we belong to God.
3. To make the marks visible, we hold the paper up to the light. Christians walk in the light.

Conclusion: Do you have a watermark?

Does this look like a plain, empty piece of paper? It's not. When I hold it up to the light, I can see some marks. This one says "Erasable Bond." You can't see the mark? That's because it is a watermark, not an ink mark. Paper is made from wood pulp, sometimes with linen or other fibers added. It is mostly water until it is squeezed between heavy rollers. The end roller for special paper like this has a raised mark that is rolled over the paper and leaves a nearly invisible print.

People who are baptized have a watermark, too. Water is used in baptism and, therefore, we can say that it leaves a watermark.

These different papers that I have with me are marked with a brand or a code name or number. Each company has its own way of marking its products. The Christian is baptized "in the name of the Father, the Son, and the Holy Spirit." This is his trademark. He belongs to the family of God.

In order to see the watermark on this paper clearly, you must hold the paper up to the light. The paper is slightly thinner where the raised mark pressed into it. That allows more light to pass through the paper. Jesus is the light of the world. When we baptize a child, we promise to hold him or her up to the light—to teach him about God's love and rear him in a Christian way. When an adult is baptized, he promises to walk in the light—to live in a close relationship with Jesus. Then the watermark will show. Do you have a watermark?

24 The Lord's Supper

Object: A photo album.

Lesson: Jesus gave us the Lord's Supper or Communion to remind us that he died for us.

Text: ". . . that the Lord Jesus, on the night he was betrayed, took a piece of bread, gave thanks to God, broke it, and said, 'This is my body, which is for you. Do this in memory of me'" (I Cor. 11:23b–24).

Outline

Introduce object: This is our family photo album. It will help me explain about the Lord's Supper or Communion.

1. Old pictures—looking back at Jesus' sacrifice for us.
2. Recent pictures—thinking about what Jesus means in our lives now.
3. Blank pages—promising to live better lives in the future.

Conclusion: Jesus gave us these symbols to help us ponder the past, pray for the present, and promise for the future.

This is our family photo album. It will help me explain about the Lord's Supper or Communion. I enjoy looking through the old pictures and thinking about people and events. The Lord's Supper is a time for looking back. Jesus told his followers to eat the broken bread and to drink the wine to remember him. When we celebrate the Lord's Supper we are looking back and remembering Jesus' sacrifice for our sins.

I also enjoy looking at recent pictures in the photo album. Sometimes I show these pictures to others so they can see what our friends and relatives look like or where they live. The Lord's Supper is also a time to think about the present. We confess things we have done wrong and ask Jesus to forgive us. We thank him and think about how to love and serve him more now.

This photo album has blank pages for pictures I haven't taken yet. There are many pictures I would like to take. There are places I will be going and things I will be doing that I will want to record on film. The Lord's Supper is also a time for thinking about the future, for promising to live more complete Christian lives, and for planning to live lives of gratitude for what Jesus did for us.

The Lord's Supper is a special time when we eat the broken bread to remind us of Jesus' body, which was broken for us, and drink the wine to remind us of Jesus' blood as he bled heavily on the cross. Jesus gave us these symbols to help us ponder the past, pray for the present, and promise for the future.

25 The Greatness of God

Object: A cordless telephone, a walkie-talkie, a CB radio, or other means of cordless communication.

Lesson: God is omnipotent, omnipresent, and omniscient.

Text: "Remember how great is God's power" (Job 36:22a). "We cannot fully know his greatness" (Job 36:26a).

Outline

Introduce object: It amazes me that there can be a telephone without a cord.

1. God is all-powerful. He isn't tied to ordinary things.
2. God is everywhere present. He can answer at any time.
3. God knows everything. He knows when you want to talk to him.

Conclusion: What a powerful God we have—and I used to think this little phone is amazing.

It amazes me that there can be a telephone without a cord. This telephone does have to be used within a specific distance from the small receiver to which it belongs, and it is set up and registered to ring with a certain number—but there is no cord and it actually works like a regular phone.

This telephone works because it follows certain scientific principles. God is the creator of these principles. Not only is he not tied to ordinary things, but he can go beyond even the scientific principles he established. Our God who can create and work miracles can certainly listen to and care for us. Our God is all-powerful.

Why make a phone without a cord? This phone can be used anywhere in the house. You can even use it in the yard. You don't have to go to the phone to answer it. You can take the phone with you. God is present everywhere. You don't have to be in your house or yard to reach him. Since he does not have a limited range, he will always be wherever you are and he will always be available for you.

When the little buzzer rings, you answer the phone. There is a dial to use when you make a call. God is just a call away from us. Better yet, because he knows everything, he knows when you want to talk to him. He knows when you need him. He is ready for your call.

What a powerful God we have—and I used to think that this little phone is amazing.

26 Forgiveness

Object: Two identical glass containers filled with specially prepared gelatin. Use a three-ounce package of gelatin, following the directions on the package. Pour two-thirds of the gelatin mixture into one of the glass containers. Add one-third cup of water to the remaining gelatin so it will not set. Pour this mixture into the other glass container.

Lesson: God forgives and forgets. He wants us to do the same.

Text: "If you kept a record of our sins, who could escape being condemned? But you forgive us, so that we should reverently obey you" (Ps. 130:3–4). "And then he says, 'I will not remember their sins and evil deeds any longer'" (Heb. 10:17).

Outline

Introduce object: I have two interesting-looking glasses with me to help me tell you about forgiveness. Pretend these glasses are two people.

1. This person is not forgiving. (Put a finger in the firm gelatin and it will leave a hole.)

2. This person is forgiving because forgiving means forgetting. (Put a finger in the other mixture and the hole will smooth over when the finger is removed.)

Conclusion: Are you a truly forgiving person?

I have two interesting-looking glasses with me to help me tell you about forgiveness. Pretend these glasses are two people. They are the same size, shape, and color, but they *are* different. One knows about true forgiveness; the other doesn't. This one is not forgiving. He is stiff and firm. When I poke my finger into this mixture and pull it out, it leaves a hole. You can say you are sorry to this person and he will say "OK," but the hole will stay. He will remember what you did.

This other person is willing to make an extra effort not only to forgive but also to forget. When I poke my finger into this mixture and pull it back out, the hole is filled in, smoothed over, forgotten. When you say you are sorry it is as if you never did what caused the harm in the first place. You are completely forgiven because all trace, all memory, is erased.

What kind of forgiveness does God offer us? The Bible tells us that he forgives and forgets completely. His special love for us makes this possible. Jesus' sacrifice for us on the cross makes forgiveness real.

How do you think God wants us to forgive? Can we just say "OK" or do we need to make an extra effort to forget? God makes the extra effort for us and he expects us to do the same. He will help us to forgive. Are you a truly forgiving person?

27 Which Is the Real Egg?

Object: A white egg, a brown egg, colored eggs, and a specially prepared egg. Soak a raw egg in vinegar overnight. A chemical reaction softens the shell and makes it feel spongy. The egg, however, remains unharmed. A bowl or other container.

Lesson: Salvation comes from the heart.

Text: "And pray that Christ will make his home in your hearts through faith" (Eph. 3:17a).

Outline

Introduce object: Which of these eggs are real?

1. If you examine the eggs from the outside you may guess but can't be sure.
2. When you check the inside, you discover that all of the eggs are real.

Conclusion: What are you like on the inside?

Which of these eggs are real? Is a brown one as good as a white one? How about these colored ones? They are all shaped like eggs. They feel like eggs. However, they do look different! I have one more egg here. It's the right size for an egg but when I squeeze it gently, it feels spongy. The shell is not hard like the others. Do you think it could be a real egg?

How can you tell if people are real Christians? Is it possible for people to sit in church with their hands folded or call themselves Christians without being Christians in their hearts? Salvation—believing God, loving and trusting him, wanting to serve him—comes from the heart. A heart that is given to God is a Christian one. It is not the color or size or shape on the outside that makes a person a Christian.

The inside. . . . Do you suppose the only way to tell for sure which eggs are real is to look at the inside? Well, I guess that means cracking them to see if they have a yolk and egg white inside of them. Let's get to the heart of the matter. How many of you think the white one is real? Yes, when I crack it open you can see the egg white and yolk. How about the brown one? Yes. Now for the colored ones. These are real, too. It looks like I will be having scrambled eggs for supper. Surely this spongy egg can't be real. I can't even crack it. I have to squeeze it open. Look at that! It is a real egg, too.

How do you tell a real Christian? You need to look, as God does, at the inside. If a person has faith in God he is indeed a real Christian. What are you like on the inside?

28 Everyone in His Place

Object: A test tube or tall glass container. Equal parts of salad or cooking oil, colored water, and syrup in separate containers. When these ingredients are poured together and shaken gently, they will mix, then settle to separate ingredients again. Hint: pour in the water and oil first, as the syrup clings to the bottom of the container. The harder you shake the mixture, the longer it will take to settle. Principle: the compound having the greatest density will sink to the bottom.

Lesson: Everyone has a place to serve, a talent to offer.

Text: "So we are to use our different gifts in accordance with the grace that God has given us" (Rom. 12:6a).

Outline

Introduce object: Everyone here is unique, different, special. Pretend these containers with different colored liquids are three different people.

1. Just as there are differences in these liquids, so are there differences in people. (Show the liquids.)

2. As the liquids are poured together, so are we together working in a group, in the same place, for the same goals. (Pour the liquids together and shake gently.)

3. The individual differences remain. People are given different gifts so they can make their own contributions. (Allow the mixture to settle.)

Conclusion: Be willing to let God use you.

Everyone here is unique, different, special. Pretend these containers with different colored liquids are three different people. They are different in color and texture, just as people are different in looks and personality. God made them that way. This world would be very dull if everyone were exactly alike.

I'm going to pour these liquids together. We'll pretend that they are meeting just as we are. We are working together, in the same place, for the same goals. We help each other and sometimes we get all mixed up and blended, as these liquids do when I shake them.

Do you see what is happening when I hold this container still? The liquids are beginning to settle. You can see them just as they were before, except that they are stacked on top of each other in this container. Even though they were mixed, they are separating and becoming distinct again. Each person is separate and important to the group because each person has something special to give, such as singing, speaking, thinking up things to do, organizing material, keeping things running smoothly, or showing concern for others. Each person has a place to serve, a gift to give, a talent to share.

The saying "A place for everything and everything in its place" goes for people, too. Everyone has something to offer. Be willing to let God use you.

29 Paper Trees

Object: A paper tree. To make a paper tree, lay about six sheets of newspaper lengthwise, overlapping them almost halfway. Roll the sheets from the short end. During the presentation, make three or four cuts, about three inches deep, from the top; bend back. Holding the bottom of the tube, place fingers in the top of the tube and pull gently.

Lesson: The Christian life is one of living, growing, changing, becoming fuller.

Text: "But continue to grow in the grace and knowledge of our Lord and Savior Jesus Christ" (II Peter 3:18).

Outline

Introduce object: Do you think I can make a paper tree out of this roll of newspapers?

1. Even though we don't usually think of it as such, our faith is living.

2. Just as this paper tree appears to be growing, so our faith should be growing.

3. As the tree is changing, becoming fuller and taller, so our Christian faith should be increasing in depth, knowledge, mercy, and good will toward others.

Conclusion: How well is your faith? Is it growing?

Do you think I can make a paper tree out of this roll of newspapers? I'll make a few cuts here and there. Now watch me pull this paper out. Of course, this isn't a living tree, but we do have something that is living, even though we don't usually think of it as such. That is our faith. It is living because it is something that should be changing, growing, reaching out to others, becoming bigger.

This paper tree appears to be growing as I pull the paper up and out. In fact, I can stretch it to quite a height if I am careful. Just how much can our faith grow? There is no end. It should always be growing, learning, and searching.

The paper tree becomes fuller as I expand it. I started with four branches and now must have more than a dozen. More and more emerge as I expand it. So, too, our Christian life becomes fuller, richer, more filled with knowledge, love, mercy, and good will toward others.

Faith is not something that comes in a neat little package that stays the same. It is living, growing, changing, becoming fuller and richer. How well is your faith? Is it growing?

30 The Prints We Leave Behind

Object: A drawing or a picture of a fingerprint or an object that has been dusted for fingerprints.

Lesson: We influence the lives we touch.

Text: ". . . and you will be witnesses for me in Jerusalem, in all of Judea and Samaria, and to the ends of the earth" (Acts 1:8).

Outline

Introduce object: Do you know that whatever you touch with your fingers is marked by an invisible print?

1. Our lives touch other people's lives daily.
2. Our touch leaves an invisible mark on people's lives.
3. This mark influences other people. It can be a good witness for what God means in our lives.

Conclusion: The love of Jesus shines in and through what we do—when we touch, when we talk, when we help—and leaves a mark of love.

Do you know that whatever you touch with your fingers is marked by an invisible print? The print looks something like this. Each print is just different enough for a detective to tell if you have touched an object. Usually we cannot see the print, but it can be dusted with a special powder to make it visible. Sometimes a thief is caught because his fingerprints have been found at the scene of a crime.

Do you know that your life touches other people's lives daily and leaves an invisible print? When you speak to someone, you touch his life. You can make people happy with a cheerful word or sad with unkind words. You can bring help or comfort to people or you can make them unhappy by a thoughtless word or action. Even when we are not thinking about it, our words and actions influence other people's lives.

The mark you leave on people's lives is invisible because that mark is on their thoughts and feelings. Sometimes the mark is made visible by their actions or words. You can be "caught" doing something helpful or harmful. Sometimes it is not until years later that we find out what an influence we have had on a person's life.

This invisible influence on a person can change his life. You can leave your mark by telling people about what God means in your life. You can let them know Jesus loves them. Your words and actions can be a witness to what loving Jesus means. You can let them know how Jesus can help them.

The love of Jesus shines in and through what we do— when we touch, when we talk, when we help—and leaves a mark of love.

31 The Power of the Holy Spirit

(Pentecost)

Object: Clothing (especially synthetic fabrics dried in an electric dryer) that clings together with static electricity. (Balloons that have been rubbed through hair or with a piece of wool can also be used.)

Lesson: The Holy Spirit is a powerful force in our lives.

Text: "But the Spirit produces love, joy, peace, patience, kindness, goodness, faithfulness" (Gal. 5:22; also read Acts 2:1–4).

Outline

Introduce object: I have a sleeper here that seems to be quite attached to these socks.

1. The Holy Spirit exerts a pull on our lives.

2. The Holy Spirit holds people together through his fruits.

3. The Holy Spirit works in us to help and support us.

Conclusion: The power of the Holy Spirit is still with us and around us all of the time. We need to use it to let it help us live better Christian lives.

I have a sleeper here that seems to be quite attached to these socks. In fact, when I try to pull the socks away, an invisible force—static electricity—pulls them back again. We have an invisible force in our lives—the power of the Holy Spirit. The power of the Holy Spirit exerts a pull on our lives. When we pull away or wander off, the Holy Spirit pulls us back. The Holy Spirit exerts a powerful force toward positive Christian living. When we cannot find the strength to follow through, the Holy Spirit gives it to us. He pulls us toward God's love. He gives us peace and joy.

These socks, when I can get them free of the sleeper, cling to each other. The static electricity is still at work. As our text says, the Holy Spirit produces the love, patience, kindness, and faithfulness we need for close Christian friendships. The Holy Spirit's power helps us to care for each other, to help each other, to fellowship and worship together. It gives us a feeling of closeness.

This sleeper can hold these socks up. It supports them without my having to hold them. The Holy Spirit works in us to help and support us in our dailing living. He helps us put biblical principles into practice. He keeps us from falling on our faces.

Pentecost is the time of year when we especially remember when the Holy Spirit came to the early believers (Acts 2:1-4). He was a powerful force in their lives. The power of the Holy Spirit is still with us and around us all of the time. We need to use it to let it help us live better Christian lives.

32 Be a Winner!

Object: A trophy or certificate for winning a team sport.

Lesson: God created you as a worthwhile person who is on this earth for a purpose.

Text: ". . . love your neighbor as you love yourself. I am the LORD" (Lev. 19:18b).

Outline

Introduce object: How many of you have ever won a trophy?

1. Dedication.

2. Confidence.

3. Teamwork.

Conclusion: Winning is a great feeling, but you don't have to have a trophy to prove that you are a winner. A confident, dedicated Christian life will have its own rewards. God created you as a worthwhile person who is on this earth for a purpose.

How many of you have ever won a trophy? This trophy belongs to my son Peter. His soccer team won it. Let's think about what went into winning this trophy. It's much like living a Christian life.

An important part of winning is dedication to the goal of playing well. You will not be a good player if you are only half-interested in the game. You need to train, work hard, and pay attention to what you are doing. It is true of Christian living that you need to be dedicated to Jesus and train yourself to work toward Christian goals.

You can't play well if you don't have any confidence in your ability to play. You will duck away from the ball, stumble over the field, and get in the way of the other players. In a similar way, God wants his people to know that they are created in his image, that they are put on this earth for a purpose, and that they can accomplish something worthwhile for him. Without this confidence, Christians might stumble helplessly around without ever getting much accomplished, or be so wrapped up in what they can't do that they are unable to do.

Of course, you won't get far as a team unless you use teamwork—help each other to score points. Teamwork is just as important in Christian living. We are to love and help our neighbors as we do ourselves. Winning is a great feeling, but you don't have to have a trophy to prove that you are a winner. A confident, dedicated Christian life will have its own rewards. God created you as a worthwhile person who is on this earth for a purpose.

33 People Are Not Good to Eat!

Object: A stuffed toy tiger, or a poster, a picture, or a drawing of a tiger.

Lesson: The best way to avoid bad habits is never to start them in the first place.

Text: "So get rid of every filthy habit and all wicked conduct" (James 1:21a). "I will show you my faith by my actions" (James 2:18b).

Outline

Introduce object: Most tigers don't eat men; they don't taste good.

1. Most bad habits are started by taking the easy way out, just as tigers resort to eating people only when they are too old or too sick to catch anything else.
2. People get used to—become addicted to—their habits, just as a tiger learns to like the taste of man.
3. The habit takes over and gets the best of people, just as a tiger's habit finally gets him (man kills him).

Conclusion: The best way to avoid a bad habit is to stay strong and not take the easy way out. Don't start in the first place. The best way to get a good habit is to begin practicing it.

Most tigers don't eat men; they don't taste good. A tiger won't go after a man unless it is too old or too weak to catch better-tasting prey. Catching a person is the easiest way to get a meal and a poor meal is better than none. Most habits are started by taking the easy way out. For example, it is easier to drop clothes on the floor than to hang them up. It is easier to grab some junk food than to think of something healthy to eat. It is easier to say that you will do something when you can get around to it than to get up and do it.

After a tiger eats a person he gets used to the taste and even begins to like it. Then he is known as a man-eating tiger. Bad habits, such as smoking, taste terrible at first, but the person gets used to it, gets to like it, and then becomes addicted to it. He is hooked on smoking the way the tiger is hooked on eating men.

Eventually the man-eating tiger is killed by his bad habit— men chase and kill him. Now, we don't shoot children for throwing their clothes on the floor, but they eventually have a big mess to clean up, get grounded or yelled at, or find they have nothing to wear. When a bad habit gets the better of us, it can be very difficult to change or stop.

The best way to avoid a bad habit is to stay strong and not take the easy way out. Don't start in the first place. The best way to get a good habit is to begin practicing it.

34 Don't Feed the Bears

Object: One or more stuffed toy bears, or a poster, a picture, or a drawing of bears.

Lesson: The Bible cautions us about temptations.

Text: "Keep watch and pray that you will not fall into temptation. The spirit is willing, but the flesh is weak" (Matt. 26:41).

Outline

Introduce object: We have several cute, cuddly-looking stuffed toy bears around our house.

1. Some things or events, like bears, appear to be friendly or innocent.

2. Our national parks have signs that say "Don't feed the bears" because bears are potentially dangerous. So are many situations we face.

Conclusion: Beware of the bears—the real ones, that is—and avoid the innocent-appearing things in our lives that can take over and keep us from being the kind of persons God wants us to be.

We have several cute, cuddly-looking stuffed toy bears around our house. Since bears are plump and friendly-looking, many manufacturers make stuffed copies of them for us to play with and enjoy. I still have this teddy bear that I saved from when I was young.

Bears really are not friendly. They are not even harmless. There are many situations facing us that appear to be innocent, or are made to seem so by others. These situations tempt us to get involved in something that may be harmful or not Christian. Can you think of some examples? Perhaps you are tempted to go along with a group that is doing something, in the name of fun, that you know is not right.

Our national parks have signs that say "Don't feed the bears." This is because bears have been known to attack people who have gotten too close. Bears are wild, dangerous animals that can be uncontrollable in the presence of people and food. The Bible warns us about temptations—things that appear innocent or fun but are not. Temptations are things that we can get carried away with, things that keep us from living a happy Christian life. Gossip is an example. We can do a great deal of harm when we say things about other people. Even the truth can easily be bent to become unkind and harmful. Another example is leaving others out of our group. We just don't think that they might be hurt by our unkind or thoughtless actions. Yet another example is that of our getting so involved with an idea or project that it uses up all the energy we should be using to do something else. The Bible warns us about things that would tempt us away from the life Jesus wants us to live.

Beware of the bears—the real ones, that is—and avoid the innocent-appearing things in our lives that can take over and keep us from being the kind of persons God wants us to be.

This book is

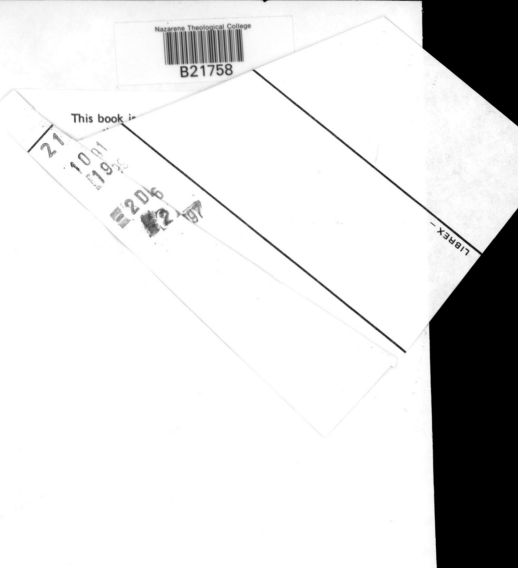